COME OUT

Elliott Doral Farmer, Jr.

COME OUT

Holiness is Right

By

Elliott Doral Farmer, Jr.

Disclaimer

This book is not meant for entertainment! If you are 12 and over reading this book, you are now held accountable for its content.

Copyright

Title book: COME OUT

Author book: Elliott Doral Farmer, Jr.

© 2018, Elliott Doral Farmer, Jr. / publisher

Self-publishing

elliottfarmerjr@gmail.com

ISBN: 978-0-9998943-2-3

ALL RIGHTS RESERVED. This book contains material protected under International and Federal Copyright Laws and Treaties. Any unauthorized reprint or use of this material is prohibited. No part of this book may be reproduced or transmitted in any form or by any means, electronic or mechanical, including photocopying, recording, or by any information storage and retrieval system without express written permission from the author/publisher.

Dedicated to ...

God the Father

God the Son (Jesus Christ)

God the Holy Ghost & Holy Spirit

To my father for ministerial training, my mother for support, my brother for having my back, and to Team Jesus Ministries, Inc.

Ephesians 4:4-6 King James Version (KJV)

4 There is one body, and one Spirit, even as ye are called in one hope of your calling;

5 One Lord, one faith, one baptism,

6 One God and Father of all, who is above all, and through all, and in you all.

Table of Contents

Preface 1

Chapter 1 15
    End Time Prophetic Revelation ....

Chapter 2 31
    Holiness: ....
    A Holy Church...

Chapter 3 48
    Satanic: ....
    Satan's Pulpit..

Chapter 4 59
    Satan's Agenda: ....
    New World Order..

Ephesians 6:10-12 King James Version (KJV) 59

Matthew 24 King James Version (KJV) 62

Chapter 5 75
    God's Agenda: ....
    New Jerusalem ....

Chapter 6 89
    Salvation & Deliverance...

PREFACE

Elliott Doral Farmer, Jr. was born on June 10, 1998. Elliott accepted Christ at age 7 in his 2nd grade classroom and received the infilling of the Holy Ghost at age 10. During this time, Elliott started preaching in 2008, and accepted his calling to ministry in 2010. Elliott has won many oratorical and ministry awards over spans of time, as well as serving on many boards as the head youth leader and youth/young adult director. In 2014, Elliott was asked to be a part of Willie P. Moore, Jr.'s SWAG TOUR as a youth ambassador.

He also won the 2014 Outstanding Youth in Ministry Award at the Full Gospel Baptist Church International Conference. Elliott has directed and appointed the president for many Gospel Choirs such as Chapel Hill High School and The University of West Georgia United Voices Gospel Choir. In 2013, Elliott Farmer, Jr. created a 4-year mentoring program called Project Black Role Model while in high school: equipping males to be role models in their communities as well as learning themselves spiritually. In March 2016, Elliott was a finalist award recipient for the 5th Annual Colored Rocks Foundation Prize in

Atlanta, Georgia for Project Black Role Model. In 2014, Elliott created a YouTube Channel entitled Fully Redeemed Broadcast. In August 2017, Elliott was appointed to serve as the President of the University of West Georgia Chapter of Team Jesus Ministries Incorporated, being the 1st Successor to the Executive President while attending the university. Elliott Farmer, Jr. has been honored and still is with different accolades. Currently, Elliott is the Executive Administrator for Team Jesus Ministries, Inc., and is the founder of The Baptostolic Movement - Philosophical Theology. He is a preacher, teacher, elocutionist, and Gospel choir director: "The New Age Prophet Elijah."

The name Elliott is the Greek form of the Hebrew Elijah, meaning Jehovah is God - my God is Jehovah.

Malachi 4:5-6 Amplified Bible (AMP)

5 "Behold, I am going to send you Elijah the prophet before the coming of the great and terrible day of the Lord.

6 He will turn the hearts of the fathers to their children, and the hearts of the children to their fathers [a reconciliation produced by repentance],

so that I will not come and strike the land with a curse [of complete destruction]."

The vision of Elliott Doral Farmer, Jr. is to help bring change to this generation. We are living in a day and time where young people are going to graves faster than the seasoned citizens. Previous generations suffered, fell, got up, and this continued to be the average cycle. This generation needs to stop lying down but needs to rise and claim victory. A new age and time have been bestowed upon us. Too many souls want to be the designated line leader but hardly anyone wants to follow. Let us finally come together as one to change a generation, and generations to come.

The book you have now embarked upon discusses what is to come concerning the saved and unsaved in a strategic, homiletical exegeses format with analysis being scripturally based.

No one is perfect; however, we should strive to be Christ-like. God is not an author of confusion, and to be unconfused, you must approach things in decency and in order. Read **1 Corinthians 14: 33-40**. Holiness is still right church. We will bust hell wide open like the rich man in **Luke 16** if we do not learn how to properly handle and treat each other as Children of God.

1 Chronicles 16:22 King James Version (KJV)

22 Saying, Touch not mine anointed, and do my prophets no harm.

1 Corinthians 15:33-34 King James Version (KJV)

33 Be not deceived: evil communications corrupt good manners.

34 Awake to righteousness, and sin not; for some have not the knowledge of God: I speak this to your shame.

It took much prayer and consecration for me to compose on paper what thus saith the Lord to help this generation we live in today. I am anointed to operate in deliverance and to discern spirits. Jesus is calling us to repentance before His return. We must start being wise and maintain our oil like the wise virgins in **Matthew 25:1-13**.

Come Out explains in a mature way of the Great Tribulation and the Millennium Reign of Christ for all audiences due to discussing the mindset of being a sinner. I highly suggest to all to pray and consecrate yourself while reading this novel. Satan may try to attack you and keep you from knowing the truth about God's Word un-sugarcoated. Please understand after reading this novel, the Lord will hold you accountable for you have been warned by His vessel on what is to come.

Luke 12:47-48 King James Version (KJV)

47 And that servant, which knew his lord's will, and prepared not himself, neither did according to his will, shall be beaten with many stripes.

The purpose and intent of this novel are to prepare and save souls for the Second Coming of Christ before the devils are loose to roam the earth in bodily form instead of as spirits influencing human flesh.

My prayer is by the time you finish this novel, you will be saved all over again, or even saved with it being your very first-time learning about Jesus Christ, as well as for Christ to speak and reveal unto you fresh revelation about the Kingdom of God at hand.

"Lord, use me as your vessel. Hide me in you that all will just see Your glory deep down within me. Let Your Word be thine lamp in my pathway. Forever give me a new prayer, praise, and worship. I want you. I need You. I have You. Selah."

- EFARMERJR

Proverbs 4:7 King James Version (KJV)

7 Wisdom is the principal thing; therefore get wisdom: and with all thy getting get understanding.

Chapter 1

End Time Prophetic Revelation

Disclaimer

If you did not read the Preface, you may want to.

God is not a toy that is to be played with whenever you want to. For instance, you cannot call yourself a pastor, yet you marry the woman you cheated on your wife with, and she becomes the new first lady in your church. We see preachers dressing up as prostitutes and hoes in the streets. Gospel artists creating songs without mentioning the birth, burial, and resurrection of Jesus Christ. God is not pleased with homosexuals being ordained as Apostles and Bishops. God is not pleased with church properties being ran like markets in the synagogues. God is tired of the embezzlement scandals or the false prophets manipulating His children deliberately for personal gain. Jesus came to bring life. Not to appoint clergy members to abuse their titles to get their conniving ways approved by man. Gospel music should not be twerked to. Preaching should not be about who can whoop the most and slain the most people out in a service. It should not be all that is done within a service is shouting, and no one leaves with a penetrated Word from heaven to change lives. Why is there so much confrontation between denominations to where confusion resides pertaining to how to explain God's Holy Word?! It is amazing to see Christians talk about holiness yet choose not to live and practice what they preach to others. The church at this point will be the main section in hell due to falsifying the Word of Truth. The church needs to realize at some point we are doing something wrong because most of our congregants are headed down the path of destruction based upon our laxness in studying the Word of God to an exegesis point of thorough presentation. The Body of Christ needs to wake up and understand that Satan is ready to tear you up and to chew you up as raw meat.

1 Peter 5:8 King James Version (KJV)

8 Be sober, be vigilant; because your adversary the devil, as a roaring lion, walketh about, seeking whom he may devour:

The devil is out here stealing, killing, and destroying, yet, the church wants to sit here and not prepare the Saints for the End Time Revelation.

Matthew 24:3-31 King James Version (KJV)

3 While he was sitting on the Mount of Olives, the disciples approached him privately, saying: "Tell us, when will these things be, and what will be the sign of your presence and of the conclusion of the system of things?"

4 In answer Jesus said to them: "Look out that nobody misleads you,

5 for many will come on the basis of my name, saying, 'I am the Christ,' and will mislead many.

6 You are going to hear of wars and reports of wars. See that you are not alarmed, for these things must take place, but the end is not yet.

7 "For nation will rise against nation and kingdom against kingdom, and there will be food shortages and earthquakes in one place after another.

8 All these things are a beginning of pangs of distress.

9 "Then people will hand you over to tribulation and will kill you, and you will be hated by all the nations on account of my name.

10 Then, too, many will be stumbled and will betray one another and will hate one another.

11 Many false prophets will arise and mislead many;

12 and because of the increasing of lawlessness, the love of the greater number will grow cold.

13 But the one who has endured to the end will be saved.

14 And this good news of the Kingdom will be preached in all the inhabited earth for a witness to all the nations, and then the end will come.

15 "Therefore, when you catch sight of the disgusting thing that causes desolation, as spoken about by Daniel the prophet, standing in a holy placer (let the reader use discernment),

16 then let those in Ju·de′a begin fleeing to the mountains.

17 Let the man on the housetop not come down to take the goods out of his house,

18 and let the man in the field not return to pick up his outer garment.t

19 Woe to the pregnant women and those nursing a baby in those days!

20 Keep praying that your flight may not occur in wintertime nor on the Sabbath day;

21 for then there will be great tribulation such as has not occurred since the world's beginning until now, no, nor will occur again.

22 In fact, unless those days were cut short, no flesh would be saved; but on account of the chosen ones those days will be cut short.

23 "Then if anyone says to you, 'Look! Here is the Christ,' or, 'There!' do not believe it.

24 For false Christs and false prophets will arise and will perform great signs and wonders so as to mislead, if possible, even the chosen ones.

25 Look! I have forewarned you.

26 Therefore, if people say to you, 'Look! He is in the wilderness,' do not go out; 'Look! He is in the inner rooms,' do not believe it.

27 For just as the lightning comes out of the east and shines over to the west, so the presence of the Son of man will be.

28 Wherever the carcass is, there the eagles will be gathered together.

29 "Immediately after the tribulation of those days, the sun will be darkened, and the moon will not give its light, and the stars will fall from heaven, and the powers of the heavens will be shaken.

30 Then the sign of the Son of man will appear in heaven, and all the tribes of the earth will beat themselves in grief, and they will see the Son of man coming on the clouds of heaven with power and great glory.

31 And he will send out his angels with a great trumpet sound, and they will gather his chosen ones together from the four winds, from one extremity of the heavens to their other extremity.

The End Times simply in Biblical terminology means towards the end. Think of it as a closing chapter to get ready for something new.

__Prophecy__ in Biblical terms is a prediction of something someone prophesies.

__Revelation__ in Biblical terms means a fact disclosed or revealed.

God is disclosing His own nature and His purpose for mankind through the words of human intermediaries, basically, a divine disclosure revealed or realized to solute a solution to an impossible problem theologically for the manifestation of God's <u>DIVINE</u> Will and truth to His righteous people.

There is only one revelation in the Bible, hence the Book of Revelation, not revelations. However, many homiletical exegeses the text differentially to help different demographics.

The Book of Revelation or the Revelation to John occupies the central place in Christian eschatology concerning the End Time Prophetic Revelation to the Church of the Living God, consisting of these three main parts:

    I.   the Epistolary

    II. the Apocalyptic

    III. the Prophetic

Revelation 1:9-11 King James Version (KJV)

9 I John, who also am your brother, and companion in tribulation, and in the kingdom and patience of Jesus Christ, was in the isle that is called Patmos, for the word of God, and for the testimony of Jesus Christ.

10 I was in the Spirit on the Lord's day, and heard behind me a great voice, as of a trumpet,

11 Saying, I am Alpha and Omega, the first and the last: and, What thou seest, write in a book, and send it unto the seven churches which are in Asia; unto Ephesus, and unto Smyrna, and unto Pergamos, and unto Thyatira, and unto Sardis, and unto Philadelphia, and unto Laodicea.

Please adhere to what thus saith the Lord through this book, as I, one of God's servants, interpret His Word rightly dividing the word of truth as stated in **2 Timothy 2:15** to help prepare you for Jesus' Coming and the End Time Prophetic Revelation unveiling.

2 Timothy 2:15 King James Version (KJV)

15 Study to shew thyself approved unto God, a workman that needeth not to be ashamed, rightly dividing the word of truth.

Chapter 2

Holiness:
A Holy Church

2 Corinthians 6:14-18 King James Version (KJV)

14 Be ye not unequally yoked together with unbelievers: for what fellowship hath righteousness with unrighteousness? and what communion hath light with darkness?

15 And what concord hath Christ with Belial? or what part hath he that believeth with an infidel?

16 And what agreement hath the temple of God with idols? for ye are the temple of the living God; as God hath said, I will dwell in them, and walk

in them; and I will be their God, and they shall be my people.

17 Wherefore come out from among them, and be ye separate, saith the Lord, and touch not the unclean thing; and I will receive you.

18 And will be a Father unto you, and ye shall be my sons and daughters, saith the Lord Almighty.

    i.   <u>HOLINESS</u> is a verb, an action from the Hebrew term qadash meaning to be set apart and consecrated.

    ii. <u>HOLINESS</u> belongs to God the Father, and to

Christians as consecrated to God's service.

iii. <u>HOLINESS</u> is also a work of personal, gradual development.

iv. <u>HOLINESS</u> is also a part of sanctification and purification of the mind, body, and soul which belongs to God.

Leviticus 19:2: "'You shall be holy'–You shall be distinct (perushim tiheyu).

Exodus 19:6: "you shall be to Me a kingdom of priests and a holy nation (goy kadosh)."

God is calling for a holiness and righteous church. Come out from among them and be ye separate says the Lord. We have got to stop intertwining ourselves with the world as God's people. We cannot go to God's House claiming salvation yet leaving and going into the world as the world. God is calling for repentance and a Blood-Washed Church meaning the Blood of Christ Jesus covering all sin.

A person cannot call themselves saved yet watch pornography and share it with others, or not pay your tithes and offerings. You cannot call yourself holy, yet you are fornicating and committing adultery, or listening to secular music with a viscous intent to feed your spirit with fleshly desires and motives. It is questionable how a person can thank God for a production that involves profanity and obstruction against the Word of God. Even the devil knows the Lord, but that does not make Satan a **Child of God**.

Ephesians 5:19 - Speaking to yourselves in psalms and hymns and spiritual songs, singing and making melody in your heart to the Lord;

James 4:4 - Ye adulterers and adulteresses, know ye not that the friendship of the world is enmity with God? whosoever therefore will be a friend of the world is the enemy of God.

1 Corinthians 10:31 - Whether therefore ye eat, or drink, or whatsoever ye do, do all to the glory of God.

Colossians 3:16 - Let the word of Christ dwell in you richly in all wisdom; teaching and admonishing one another in psalms and hymns and spiritual songs, singing with grace in your hearts to the Lord.

2 Corinthians 6:17 - Wherefore come out from among them, and be ye separate, saith the Lord, and touch not the unclean [thing]; and I will receive you,

Philippians 4:8 - Finally, brethren, whatsoever things are true, whatsoever things [are] honest, whatsoever things [are] just, whatsoever things [are] pure, whatsoever things [are] lovely, whatsoever things [are] of good report; if [there be] any virtue, and if [there be] any praise, think on these things.

Holiness is what makes the church, God's people, unique; therefore, preachers must stop preaching holiness doctrine when they do not live and practice holiness themselves. The church has gotten so foolish in the pulpit to where homosexuality is acceptable. Nowadays, you have preachers marrying those who are not husband

and wife (man and woman). Ultimately, representing the conformalities of the world.

Leviticus 20:13 English Standard Version (ESV)

13 If a man lies with a male as with a woman, both of them have committed an abomination;

Romans 1:26-27 English Standard Version (ESV)

26 For this reason God gave them up to dishonorable passions. For their women exchanged natural relations for those that are contrary to nature;

27 and the men likewise gave up natural relations with women and were consumed with passion for one another, men committing shameless acts with men and receiving in themselves the due penalty for their error.

Hebrews 13:4-7 English Standard Version (ESV)

4 Let marriage be held in honor among all, and let the marriage bed be undefiled, for God will judge the sexually immoral and adulterous

.

Romans 12:1-3 King James Version (KJV)

1 I beseech you therefore, brethren, by the mercies of God, that ye present your bodies a living sacrifice, holy, acceptable unto God, which is your reasonable service.

2 And be not conformed to this world: but be ye transformed by the renewing of your mind, that ye may prove what is that good, and acceptable, and perfect, will of God.

3 For I say, through the grace given unto me, to every man that is among you, not to think of himself more highly than he ought to think; but to think soberly, according as God hath dealt to every man the measure of faith.

Being holy and right before God does not mean nor give you the right to condemn others. **Read Romans 8 & Romans 14.** Although God does not want us to be like the world, God wants us to still share and show the love of Christ. Holiness is still right and should not be taken likely. However, do not get so self-righteous to where you miss out on the benefits of holiness living.

Matthew 7:1-3 King James Version (KJV)

1 Judge not, that ye be not judged.

2 For with what judgment ye judge, ye shall be judged: and with what measure ye mete, it shall be measured to you again.

3 And why beholdest thou the mote that is in thy brother's eye, but considerest not the beam that is in thine own eye?

John 3:17-18 King James Version (KJV)

17 For God sent not his Son into the world to condemn the world; but that the world through him might be saved.

18 He that believeth on him is not condemned: but he that believeth not is condemned already, because he hath not believed in the name of the only begotten Son of God.

Whenever you think about holiness as a Christian, remember these simple attributes:

1. To be holy is to be distinct, separate, in a class by oneself under Hosanna being Christ.

2. To be holy is to be pure inside and out, both spiritual and in the natural in all aspects of life including the way you walk, talk and live.

3. For God to be holy is for God to be holy in the relation of every aspect in His nature, character, and anything else we are still learning about Him in His Holy Word.

4. The holiness of God should be a guide and governor to our everyday thinking on His acceptance.

5. The doctrine of God's view of holiness needs to always be considered when speaking of accountability.

6. God's holiness should govern our thinking about self-esteem.

7. The holiness of God should caution the Church about what we accept and practice from the contemporary "church growth" movement in today's societal generation.

8. Just a grasp of holiness should change how we praise and worship God through attitudinal conduct.

9. The appropriate response to the holiness of God in reverence is in the form of in working (internal) and outworking (external) obedience due to having the fear of Jehovah, God.

10. The holiness of God makes the Gospel of Jesus Christ a glorious necessity for the

Body of Christ and souls being added daily to God's Kingdom.

Chapter 3

Satanic: Satan's Pulpit

1 John 2:15-16 King James Version (KJV)

15 Love not the world, neither the things that are in the world. If any man love the world, the love of the Father is not in him.

16 For all that is in the world, the lust of the flesh, and the lust of the eyes, and the pride of life, is not of the Father, but is of the world.

Satan is a fallen angel, who is known as the deceiver of humanity. Satan is considered the devil with demons attached to him. **John 10:10** – Satan comes to steal, kill, and destroy. To understand Satan and his tactics, you first must understand the previous lifestyle of this demonic figure who is seeking whom he may devour. **Read 1 Peter 5:8**.

Before Satan became Satan, he was once known and referred to as Lucifer, who was the second archangel, meaning bright and morning star, in heaven.

Isaiah 14:12-14 King James Version (KJV)

12 How art thou fallen from heaven, O Lucifer, son of the morning! how art thou cut down to the ground, which didst weaken the nations!

13 For thou hast said in thine heart, I will ascend into heaven, I will exalt my throne above the stars of God: I will sit also upon the mount of the congregation, in the sides of the north:

14 I will ascend above the heights of the clouds; I will be like the most High.

Lucifer got full of himself and felt he could overtake God, and when God saw this, Lucifer and his followers were kicked out of God's kingdom, had name changes, and Satan created his own dynasty. In today's time, you have a lot of modern Lucifers being seen in the pulpit, and God says that He will cast it down.

Exodus 20:3-5 King James Version (KJV)

3 Thou shalt have no other gods before me.

4 Thou shalt not make unto thee any graven image, or any likeness of any thing that is in heaven above, or that is in the earth beneath, or that is in the water under the earth.

5 Thou shalt not bow down thyself to them, nor serve them: for I the Lord thy God am a jealous God, visiting the iniquity of the fathers upon the children unto the third and fourth generation of them that hate me;

Satan's motive is to get you to join his army and to go against God. Satan's kingdom is not eternal like God's. It shall not last forever because eventually, the Lord is going to cast Satan and his followers down into the bottomless pit called hell. Satan's kingdom is full of darkness, full of sin, full of misery, full of strife. No life and freedom can be found in the kingdom of Satan because, in his kingdom, you are on the track of being hell-bound. Satan's kingdom is considered as a sphere of his satanic reign. Jesus, in **John 13:30,** even calls Satan "the prince of the world." Moreover, Satan has messengers of various ranks within his kingdom called principalities, powers, rulers, dominions, and spiritual hosts of the wickedness of the air.

Ephesians 6:12 King James Version (KJV)

12 For we wrestle not against flesh and blood, but against principalities, against powers, against the rulers of the darkness of this world, against spiritual wickedness in high places.

Ephesians 2:2 King James Version (KJV)

2 Wherein in time past ye walked according to the course of this world, according to the prince of the power of the air, the spirit that now worketh in the children of disobedience:

Ephesians 1:21 King James Version (KJV)

21 Far above all principality, and power, and might, and dominion, and every name that is named, not only in this world, but also in that which is to come:

Satan is presently called the "god of the world" in 2 Corinthians 4:4. Jesus referred to Satan's Kingdom in **Matthew 12:26** when He said, "And if Satan cast out Satan, he is divided against himself; how shall then his kingdom stand?" The world and its present kingdoms are under the domain and dominion of Satan. However, one day and this day is coming soon as scripture unfolds, Jesus Christ will take away the kingdoms of this present world from Satan, and they will become the Lord's. The book of Revelation tells us, "...The kingdoms of this world are become the kingdoms of our Lord, and His Christ; and He shall reign forever and ever (**Revelation 11:15**)." But, presently, Satan has control. Furthermore, in Satan's kingdom, there are many demons, evil spirits, who serve as his servants.

The kingdom of Satan is categorized in these three groups:

1. Satan, the head

2. The fallen angels who followed Satan in rebelling against God and who served as ministers and officials to rule for him in the air.

3. The disembodied spirits, demons, and evil spirits who acted as Satan's servants to run his satanic agenda on earth.

Satan's kingdom is illegal because it was not orchestrated by the ultimate ruler and governor being God the Father. Hence why in the Lord's Prayer, Jesus says to pray for His (Jesus') kingdom to come on earth as it is alive in heaven because Satan's kingdom is swiftly coming down on earth.

Revelation 11:15 King James Version (KJV)

15 And the seventh angel sounded; and there were great voices in heaven, saying, The kingdoms of this world are become the kingdoms of our Lord, and of his Christ; and he shall reign for ever and ever.

Chapter 4

Satan's Agenda: New World Order

Ephesians 6:10-12 King James Version (KJV)

[10] Finally, my brethren, be strong in the Lord, and in the power of his might.

[11] Put on the whole armour of God, that ye may be able to stand against the wiles of the devil.

[12] For we wrestle not against flesh and blood, but against principalities, against powers, against the rulers of the darkness of this world, against spiritual wickedness in high places.

Satan is your adversary, not your brethren. You must understand as well that Satan has an agenda with levels. First, you will encounter principalities. Next, you will encounter powers. Thereafter, rulers of the darkness of this world. Lastly, spiritual wickedness in high places.

Just like Jehovah, Satan has a strategy and plan to keep you from your destiny, to keep you from obtaining all Christ wants you to obtain. The Second Coming or the Second Parousia of Jesus Christ discusses the Rapture of the Church. All those who are righteous and holy before God in His eyes shall be called to meet Jesus in the air; however, those remaining shall endure the hardships because of disobedience to God the Father.

The Abomination of Desolation will occur halfway through the final seven years, triggering the Great Tribulation Period. During this final three and one-half years, the Antichrist will move to stamp out all resistance to his authority wherever he has control. Jesus prophesied that it will be a time of tribulation such as never has been before nor ever again shall be.

MATTHEW 24 KING JAMES VERSION (KJV)

24 And Jesus went out, and departed from the temple: and his disciples came to him for to shew him the buildings of the temple.

² And Jesus said unto them, See ye not all these things? verily I say unto you, There shall not be left here one stone upon another, that shall not be thrown down.

³ And as he sat upon the mount of Olives, the disciples came unto him privately, saying, Tell us, when shall these things be? and what shall be the sign of thy coming, and of the end of the world?

⁴ And Jesus answered and said unto them, Take heed that no man deceive you.

5 For many shall come in my name, saying, I am Christ; and shall deceive many.

6 And ye shall hear of wars and rumours of wars: see that ye be not troubled: for all these things must come to pass, but the end is not yet.

7 For nation shall rise against nation, and kingdom against kingdom: and there shall be famines, and pestilences, and earthquakes, in divers places.

8 All these are the beginning of sorrows.

9 Then shall they deliver you up to be afflicted, and shall kill you: and ye shall be hated of all nations for my name's sake.

10 And then shall many be offended, and shall betray one another, and shall hate one another.

11 And many false prophets shall rise, and shall deceive many.

12 And because iniquity shall abound, the love of many shall wax cold.

13 But he that shall endure unto the end, the same shall be saved.

14 And this gospel of the kingdom shall be preached in all the world for a witness unto all nations; and then shall the end come.

15 When ye therefore shall see the abomination of desolation, spoken of by Daniel the prophet, stand in the holy place, (whoso readeth, let him understand:)

16 Then let them which be in Judaea flee into the mountains:

17 Let him which is on the housetop not come down to take any thing out of his house:

18 Neither let him which is in the field return back to take his clothes.

19 And woe unto them that are with child, and to them that give suck in those days!

20 But pray ye that your flight be not in the winter, neither on the sabbath day:

21 For then shall be great tribulation, such as was not since the beginning of the world to this time, no, nor ever shall be.

22 And except those days should be shortened, there should no flesh be saved: but for the elect's sake those days shall be shortened.

23 Then if any man shall say unto you, Lo, here is Christ, or there; believe it not.

24 For there shall arise false Christs, and false prophets, and shall shew great signs and wonders; insomuch that, if it were possible, they shall deceive the very elect.

25 Behold, I have told you before.

26 Wherefore if they shall say unto you, Behold, he is in the desert; go not forth: behold, he is in the secret chambers; believe it not.

27 For as the lightning cometh out of the east, and shineth even unto the west; so shall also the coming of the Son of man be.

28 For wheresoever the carcase is, there will the eagles be gathered together.

29 Immediately after the tribulation of those days shall the sun be darkened, and the moon shall not give her light, and the stars shall fall from heaven, and the powers of the heavens shall be shaken:

30 And then shall appear the sign of the Son of man in heaven: and then shall all the tribes of the earth mourn, and they shall see the Son of man coming in the clouds of heaven with power and great glory.

31 And he shall send his angels with a great sound of a trumpet, and they shall gather together his elect from the four winds, from one end of heaven to the other.

32 Now learn a parable of the fig tree; When his branch is yet tender, and putteth forth leaves, ye know that summer is nigh:

33 So likewise ye, when ye shall see all these things, know that it is near, even at the doors.

34 Verily I say unto you, This generation shall not pass, till all these things be fulfilled.

35 Heaven and earth shall pass away, but my words shall not pass away.

36 But of that day and hour knoweth no man, no, not the angels of heaven, but my Father only.

37 But as the days of Noah were, so shall also the coming of the Son of man be.

38 For as in the days that were before the flood they were eating and drinking, marrying and giving in marriage, until the day that Noe entered into the ark,

39 And knew not until the flood came, and took them all away; so shall also the coming of the Son of man be.

40 Then shall two be in the field; the one shall be taken, and the other left.

41 Two women shall be grinding at the mill; the one shall be taken, and the other left.

⁴² Watch therefore: for ye know not what hour your Lord doth come.

⁴³ But know this, that if the goodman of the house had known in what watch the thief would come, he would have watched, and would not have suffered his house to be broken up.

⁴⁴ Therefore be ye also ready: for in such an hour as ye think not the Son of man cometh.

⁴⁵ Who then is a faithful and wise servant, whom his lord hath made ruler over his household, to give them meat in due season?

⁴⁶ Blessed is that servant, whom his lord when he cometh shall find so doing.

⁴⁷ Verily I say unto you, That he shall make him ruler over all his goods.

48 But and if that evil servant shall say in his heart, My lord delayeth his coming;

49 And shall begin to smite his fellowservants, and to eat and drink with the drunken;

50 The lord of that servant shall come in a day when he looketh not for him, and in an hour that he is not aware of,

51 And shall cut him asunder, and appoint him his portion with the hypocrites: there shall be weeping and gnashing of teeth.

The Antichrist, Jesus says, will have become so drunk on power that he will hatch a scheme to force every person on earth to pledge his or her allegiance to him. The second beast is the false prophet which can be found mentioned in **Revelation 19:20.**

A decree will even be made for every person living to swear allegiance to the Antichrist and his one-world government or be boycotted economically. In fact, each person on earth will be issued a global identification number that will be absolutely required to hold or obtain a job, otherwise known as the Mark of the Beast as found in **Revelation 13.**

Anyone employing a person without the global ID will be branded as a subversive and an enemy of the state. Once a person cannot find a job, he will no longer be able to buy or sell and is stated to bow the knee to the New World Order or else.

The New World Order is a secret, power elite group with a globalist agenda is conspiring to eventually rule the world through an authoritarian world government. This authoritarian government is set out to replace sovereign nation-states, along with encompassing propaganda to establish the ideology of the New World Order to culminate the progression of history in the making.

Revelation 13:7 states that power will be given to the Antichrist over "all kindreds, and tongues, and nations." Verse 3 states, "And all the world wondered after the beast."

Daniel 7:23 tells of a world governmental system ruled by the Antichrist, "The fourth beast shall be the fourth kingdom upon earth, which shall be diverse from all kingdoms, and shall devour the whole earth, and shall tread it down, and break it in pieces." The prophecy then states that this world government will rule the world until the Second Coming of Jesus Christ.

Chapter 5

God's Agenda: New Jerusalem

After the second coming of Jesus Christ, once the 7 Year Tribulation Period ends, the Bible says Jesus shall take His throne and shall reign over all. New Jerusalem is considered the new place where the Saints of God shall dwell. When God's Kingdom takes place, New Jerusalem shall be in pure gold like clear glass. God gives John the Revelator in Revelation a clear depiction of what is being created for those who cross over into Heaven on Judgement Day.

New Jerusalem, this New Earth to come, the Bible says shall be free of sin and the servants of God will have theosis with Christ's Name on their foreheads. No more night shall be because the light which is Christ shall forever be shining. No more temples before all will only worship Jesus who shall sit on the Throne of God.

Revelation 21

King James Bible

A New Heaven and a New Earth

1 And I saw a new heaven and a new earth: for the first heaven and the first earth were passed away; and there was no more sea.

2 And I John saw the holy city, new Jerusalem, coming down from God out of heaven, prepared as a bride adorned for her husband.

3 And I heard a great voice out of heaven saying, Behold, the tabernacle of God is with men, and he will dwell with them, and they shall be his people, and God himself shall be with them, and be their God.

4 And God shall wipe away all tears from their eyes; and there shall be no more death, neither

sorrow, nor crying, neither shall there be any more pain: for the former things are passed away.

5 And he that sat upon the throne said, Behold, I make all things new. And he said unto me, Write: for these words are true and faithful.

6 And he said unto me, It is done. I am Alpha and Omega, the beginning and the end. I will give unto him that is athirst of the fountain of the water of life freely.

7 He that overcometh shall inherit all things; and I will be his God, and he shall be my son.

8 But the fearful, and unbelieving, and the abominable, and murderers, and whoremongers, and sorcerers, and idolaters, and all liars, shall have their part in the lake which burneth with fire and brimstone: which is the second death.

The New Jerusalem

9 And there came unto me one of the seven angels which had the seven vials full of the seven last plagues, and talked with me, saying, Come hither, I will shew thee the bride, the Lamb's wife.

10 And he carried me away in the spirit to a great and high mountain, and shewed me that great city, the holy Jerusalem, descending out of heaven from God,

11 Having the glory of God: and her light was like unto a stone most precious, even like a jasper stone, clear as crystal;

12 And had a wall great and high, and had twelve gates, and at the gates twelve angels, and names written thereon, which are the names of the twelve tribes of the children of Israel:

13 On the east three gates; on the north three gates; on the south three gates; and on the west three gates.

14 And the wall of the city had twelve foundations, and in them the names of the twelve apostles of the Lamb.

15 And he that talked with me had a golden reed to measure the city, and the gates thereof, and the wall thereof.

16 And the city lieth foursquare, and the length is as large as the breadth: and he measured the city with the reed, twelve thousand furlongs. The length and the breadth and the height of it are equal.

17 And he measured the wall thereof, an hundred and forty and four cubits, according to the measure of a man, that is, of the angel.

18 And the building of the wall of it was of jasper: and the city was pure gold, like unto clear glass.

19 And the foundations of the wall of the city were garnished with all manner of precious stones. The first foundation was jasper; the second, sapphire; the third, a chalcedony; the fourth, an emerald;

20 The fifth, sardonyx; the sixth, sardius; the seventh, chrysolite; the eighth, beryl; the ninth, a topaz; the tenth, a chrysoprasus; the eleventh, a jacinth; the twelfth, an amethyst.

21 And the twelve gates were twelve pearls; every several gate was of one pearl: and the street of the city was pure gold, as it were transparent glass.

22 And I saw no temple therein: for the Lord God Almighty and the Lamb are the temple of it.

23 And the city had no need of the sun, neither of the moon, to shine in it: for the glory of God did lighten it, and the Lamb is the light thereof.

24 And the nations of them which are saved shall walk in the light of it: and the kings of the earth do bring their glory and honour into it.

25 And the gates of it shall not be shut at all by day: for there shall be no night there.

26 And they shall bring the glory and honour of the nations into it.

27 And there shall in no wise enter into it any thing that defileth, neither whatsoever worketh abomination, or maketh a lie: but they which are written in the Lamb's book of life.

New Jerusalem is the Tabernacle of God, the Holy City foursquare in the Celestial City that only the righteous of Christ can dwell therein. New

Jerusalem is basically Heaven literally on Earth which will present Earth in a different form once Glory hits the grounds and roams.

In **Revelation 21**, you notice the history of mankind has come to an end. Every age ever name would have ended, and Christ has gathered His church in the Rapture as stated in **1 Thessalonians 4:15–17**. Along with the Rapture taking place, The Tribulation Period would have passed as stated in **Revelation 6–18**, and the battle of Armageddon would have been fought and won by our Lord Jesus Christ as written in **Revelation 19:17–21**.

In addition to the text, Satan has been chained for the 1,000-year reign of Christ on earth mentioned in **Revelation 20:1-3**, and a new, glorious temple has been established in Jerusalem as written in **Ezekiel 40–48**. Once the final rebellion against God has been quashed, Satan shall receive his just punishment, an eternity in the lake of fire mentioned in **Revelation 20:7–10**, and The Great White Throne Judgment would have taken place with mankind being judged as written in **Revelation 20:11–15**.

In **Revelation 21:1**, God completely makes over heaven and earth as Prophet Isaiah prophesied in **Isaiah 65:17**, and what Apostle Peter has stated in **2 Peter 3:12–13**. The new heaven and new earth will be again where only the righteousness can and shall dwell. New Jerusalem, in fact, is the same city that Abraham looked for in faith as mentioned in **Hebrews 11:10**. God will dwell in New Jerusalem with His people forever, and every inhabitant of the celestial city will have all their tears wiped away as found in **Revelation 21:4**.

New Jerusalem will be fantastically huge, a city nearly 1,400 miles long, and as wide and as high as it is long (**Revelation 21:15–17**). New Jerusalem will also be dazzling in every way, with its light being lighted by the glory of God. Twelve foundations will bear the names of the twelve apostles, and twelve gates will bear the names of the twelve tribes of Israel with the street made of pure gold.

New Jerusalem will be a place of unimagined blessing, and the curse of the old earth will be gone. New Jerusalem will have the tree of life for the healing of the nations, along with the river of life. New Jerusalem is the ultimate fulfillment of all God's promises, and God's goodness shall fully manifest.

Chapter 6

Salvation & Deliverance

Joshua 24:14-15 English Standard Version (ESV)

Choose Whom You Will Serve

14 "Now therefore fear the Lord and serve him in sincerity and in faithfulness. Put away the gods that your fathers served beyond the River and in Egypt, and serve the Lord.

15 And if it is evil in your eyes to serve the Lord, choose this day whom you will serve, whether the gods your fathers served in the region beyond the River, or the gods of the Amorites in whose land you dwell. But as for me and my house, we will serve the Lord."

Choose ye this day whom ye shall serve. Either serve God or Satan, but you cannot serve two masters. **John 3:16** states that God so loved us that He sent His only begotten Son, Jesus Christ, to save mankind. You must be born again to enter the gates of Heaven. Nicodemus asked Christ how one can be born again, and the response of Christ was to just believe in Him and ye shall be saved. Flee from sin and turn from your wicked ways. Repent for the time is at hand before the trumpet is to blow, and for the glory clouds to open with Jesus coming through the cracks to call up the Real Church of His as His Bride.

Repent means to turn away from sin.

2 Peter 3:9 King James Version (KJV)

9 The Lord is not slack concerning his promise, as some men count slackness; but is longsuffering to us-ward, not willing that any should perish, but that all should come to repentance.

Heaven is a place everyone wants to go. Heaven is God's dwelling place. **Revelation 21:4** talks about Heaven being an eternal place without sorrow. Heaven is the place Jesus states in **John 14:2-3** that has many mansions He is preparing for His church. However, there is a place for those who do not get saved while on earth. Hell is where many will go the Bible says due to those not accepting Christ as their Lord and Savior, as well as falsified Christians who claim to know Christ, but Christ does not know them.

Matthew 7:21-23 New King James Version (NKJV)

I Never Knew You

21 "Not everyone who says to Me, 'Lord, Lord,' shall enter the kingdom of heaven, but he who does the will of My Father in heaven.

22 Many will say to Me in that day, 'Lord, Lord, have we not prophesied in Your name, cast out demons in Your name, and done many wonders in Your name?'

23 And then I will declare to them, 'I never knew you; depart from Me, you who practice lawlessness!'

Hell is the place of souls of the wicked. Hell is a fiery furnace as stated in **Matthew 13:42**, the Lake of Fire with flames that will never go out. Hell has no rest and it is full of destruction.

Why be separated from God's presence in eternal suffering darkness?! "In flaming fire, inflicting vengeance on those who do not know God and on those who do not obey the gospel of our Lord Jesus. These will suffer the punishment of eternal destruction, separated from the presence of the Lord and from the glory of His might (**2 Thessalonians 1:8-9**)." Choose eternal life as a righteous being versus eternal punishment because of your lack of knowledge in and of Jesus Christ.

1 Corinthians 15:50 King James Version (KJV)

50 Now this I say, brethren, that flesh and blood cannot inherit the kingdom of God; neither doth corruption inherit incorruption.

If you are not saved or are a backslider and want to be saved after reading this book, recite this out loud:

Salvation is the gift of eternal life that is made possible only through Jesus Christ. **John 3:16-17 KJV** states, "For God so loved the world, that he gave his only begotten Son, that whosoever believeth in him should not perish, but have everlasting life. For God sent not his Son into the world to condemn the world; but that the world through him might be saved." By grace, I can be saved. I truly believe in my heart that Jesus Christ died for my sins and that He has raised from the dead will all power in His Hands. I do believe that Jesus will return to take me as His own. I do believe Christ sent His Holy Spirit to be my guide and comforter of peace. I have now confessed with my mouth and believed in my heart that Jesus is Lord above all. I do believe I am now saved by the Blood and Grace of Jesus Christ in Jesus' Name, Amen!

So, come out and push into your greater,

Selah!

www.ingramcontent.com/pod-product-compliance
Lightning Source LLC
Chambersburg PA
CBHW041620220426

43661CB00046B/1512